SDMS Choral Music

CONCERT CHORALS

FOR THE DEVELOPING CHOIR

3-Part Mixed or SAB Voicings for the Changing Needs of Young Singers
By Greg Gilpin

PLAYBACK+
Speed • Pitch • Balance • Loop

DIGITAL DOWNLOAD CODE
To access AUDIO MP3 and STUDENT PDFs, go to:
www.halleonard.com/mylibrary

Enter Code
4345-5123-4375-7667

  TEACHER'S NOTE
Audio Recordings and Singer PDF files are available for Digital Download when this icon is present.

The original purchaser of this book has permission to reproduce and distribute the singer songsheets, as indicated, and project the data files for educational use only. No other part of this publication may be reproduced or distributed in any form or by any means without the prior written permission of the Publisher. Any other use is strictly prohibited.

SHAWNEE PRESS

EXCLUSIVELY DISTRIBUTED BY

Copyright © 2018 by HAL LEONARD LLC
International Copyright Secured All Rights Reserved

Visit Hal Leonard Online at
www.halleonard.com

Contact us:
Hal Leonard
7777 West Bluemound Road
Milwaukee, WI 53213
Email: info@halleonard.com

In Europe, contact:
Hal Leonard Europe Limited
42 Wigmore Street
Marylebone, London, W1U 2RN
Email: info@halleonardeurope.com

In Australia, contact:
Hal Leonard Australia Pty. Ltd.
4 Lentara Court
Cheltenham, Victoria, 3192 Australia
Email: info@halleonard.com.au

TABLE OF CONTENTS

Sing a Mighty Song!.	3
Kyrie	.18
Didn't My Lord Deliver Daniel	.25
Think on Me	.38
All Night, All Day	.49
Ha Shalom.	.62
Joshua Fit the Battle	.72
So Take This Song of Joy	.77
A La Nanita Nana	.87
Let Music Live!	.95

ABOUT THE WRITER

Greg Gilpin

Greg is a well-known ASCAP award-winning choral composer and arranger with hundreds of publications to his credit. He is also in demand as a conductor for choral festivals, all-district and all-state choirs and is a member of NAfME, ACDA and Life-Loyal Member of Phi Mu Alpha Sinfonia. As Director of Educational Choral Publications for Shawnee Press, Inc., Greg oversees creation of the educational music products for this distinguished publisher.

REHEARSAL SUGGESTIONS FOR

Sing a Mighty Song!

Discuss the style and "feel" of the piece. What is it trying to convey to the listener?

What can help create energy for the piece? Consonants? Vowels? Dynamics? How and where in the piece?

Are there different musical styles in the piece? If so, where and what is the reason for these differences?

Learn the form of the piece. Learning the form will help in memorization.

There is a wealth of dynamic contrast in the piece. Discuss in each section the written dynamics and how your choir can enhance these dynamics even more.

Use the introduction of "alleluia" as a warm-up.

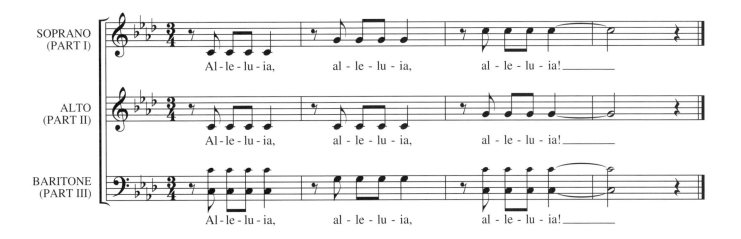

Sing a Mighty Song!

for SAB/3-Part Mixed with Piano and optional Trumpet

Words and Music by
GREG GILPIN

Copyright © 2010 by HAL LEONARD CORPORATION
This arrangement Copyright © 2018 by HAL LEONARD CORPORATION
International Copyright Secured   All Rights Reserved

REHEARSAL SUGGESTIONS FOR
Kyrie

What language is the text? What does the text mean in English. Write the English translation into the choral with pencil.

Try singing the piece on an "Oo" vowel. Work on a smooth, legato sound as you learn the intervals between notes. Then change to a "doo"

As you add the text, discover the important syllables in the words and the important words within a phrase and emphasize them by pulling back on the less important syllables and words.

Discuss when a "Kyrie" text is sung in a mass and why.

This piece was written in remembrance of a child that was born and lived only a short time. The "Oo" is the song of the child and the repetition of it at the end reflects the thought that though the child is no longer with us physically, the song of the child, the memory, the love felt will live on forever.

Use the beginning two measures of the song as a small warm-up. Try adding the next two measures of harmony to create a longer warm up, changing keys up and down.

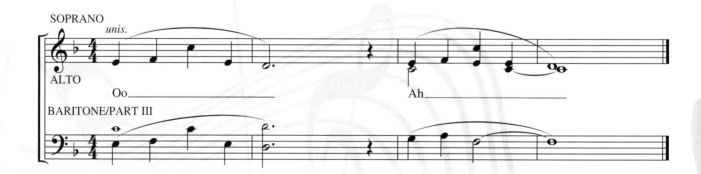

Kyrie

For SAB/3-Part Mixed with Piano and optional String Quartet

Traditional Latin Text

Music by
GREG GILPIN

Copyright © 1998 by Shawnee Press, Inc.
This arrangement Copyright © 2018 by Shawnee Press, Inc.
International Copyright Secured   All Rights Reserved

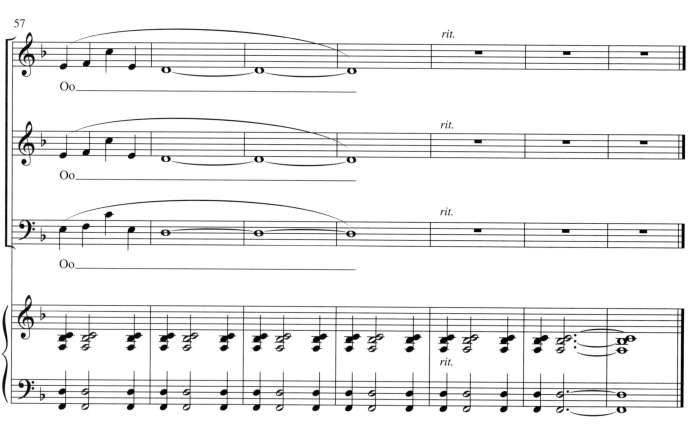

REHEARSAL SUGGESTIONS FOR
Didn't My Lord Deliver Daniel?

Discuss the text. What musical genre is this song? What is the history of this song?

Discuss the form of the piece. Each verse is a story. From where did the stories come?

Give each singer an index card. As you sing and whenever there is a rest, flick the index card. Is everyone making a sound at the same time? If not, why? Learn where the rests are and learn that the rests give the next entrance energy.

Try flicking the index cards on certain consonants. Try a D. Discover the rhythmic phrase created when flicking the cards on a D consonant.

Everyone should learn the descant at some point. Use it as a warm-up by starting on a lower note or key. Pop the consonants, find the rests, make it all very clean and sharp.

Here is challenging warm-up that will help solidify the ending. Here it is in the original key. Try going down a few steps and back up a few steps to really learn these two measures and the different contrasting rhythms that are happening between vocal parts. Then sing the final "man" the last time.

Didn't My Lord Deliver Daniel?

For SAB/3-Part Mixed with Piano

Traditional Spiritual

Arranged by
GREG GILPIN

Copyright © 2013 by HAL LEONARD CORPORATION
This arrangement Copyright © 2018 by HAL LEONARD CORPORATION
International Copyright Secured   All Rights Reserved

REHEARSAL SUGGESTIONS FOR
Think on Me

Who is "Alicia Ann Scott"? Have everyone research the poet and composer.

Discuss the text at length. Who are we singing about? What is the situation? How does this apply today and within the lives of the singers?

Is this piece full of rhythmic energy or more legato? What are ways a singer can create a legato sound but still enunciate the text?

Try having singers find a partner and each stand facing each other, holding each other's right wrist. Now pull just enough that the other has to pull equal strength. As you are pulling, sing the piece. This will create a legato sound the singers will FEEL as well as hear. Now create that sound without the physical exercise.

Work on the phrase "think on me", connecting the "k" of "think" to "on" without a space in between.

Remember to not sing too loudly but work on phrasing and dynamics without too much sound. Save the forte for measure 42.

What happens at Measure 50? What is different here? This should be sung more hymn-like. What does that mean to your singers? At measure 58, the style changes out of the hymn-like sound. What does one do to create a different style now?

The last measures, what is different with the phrase "think on me"? Are there rests added? If so, sing the phrases and emphasize the rests with the "k" sound of "think".

Strive for a tall "e" sound for "me" at the end. Try using a more "Oo" vowel shape to the lips as an "e" is sung.

REHEARSAL SUGGESTIONS FOR

All Night, All Day
(A Gospel Setting)

Discuss and listen to other examples of this song. What are the other styles? What style is this piece and how is it different?

What is the form of the piece?

There is choreography to this song. Try learning the movement as you learn the piece. Does it help give you energy? Does it help you sing the notes? Does it help with memorization?

In what key does this piece begin? Where is the key change and what is the new key? Why do you think there is a key change?

Many gospel choirs add claps to their performance. Learn how to clap together, cleanly and without covering up your voices. Try clapping your fingers on the heel of your palms instead of the center. Use lots of energy to "show" the clapping instead of lots of sound that can become sloppy rhythmically.

Beginning with measure 34 through 49, learn and sing this as a warm-up.

Using these two phrases moving up and down in keys, work on diction and singing the quarter rests with a strong "t" and "y" of "night" and "day". Which one is a hard consonant and which is a soft?

Continue up and down scale as desired

*The piano should enter on beat 1.5 with the sixteenth notes in the RH.

REHEARSAL SUGGESTIONS FOR
Ha Shalom

What language is used for this piece? Do you know any other songs in this language?

What is the English translation? Try writing the translations within the choral, if needed.

What instrument is used in addition to the piano in the accompaniment? Why do you think this instrument is used?

Once the text is established, try singing without consonants. Think about the vowels and keeping them open. Then add the consonants. This will be a challenge.

Beginning at measure 67, pay attention to the text and the change that happens at measure 71. Rehearse this section many times to establish and solidify this section. It can be tricky if not memorized immediately.

Try this a fun warm-up and musical challenge:

Looking at the violin part, sing an octave lower (in the vocal range) and learn what the violin is playing. This will be a fun challenge. Perhaps each section can take a turn and see who sings it the most correctly! Or soloists!

Ha Shalom

For SAB/3-Part Mixed with Piano and optional Violin

Traditional Hebrew*

Music by
GREG GILPIN

*Translation: *Ha shalom le maan ha amin* Peace shall be for all the world.
Ha amin le maan ha shalom All the world shall be for peace.

Copyright © 2003, 2004 by Shawnee Press, Inc.
This arrangement Copyright © 2018 by Shawnee Press, Inc.
International Copyright Secured   All Rights Reserved

REHEARSAL SUGGESTIONS FOR
Joshua Fit the Battle

Is this piece swung or even eighth notes?

What other examples can you present that the style is different or the same as this arrangement?

What kind of feeling does straight eighth notes create instead of swung?

Share some history about the song.

Try switching parts. Let the men sing the soprano line and let the women sing the men's line.

Circle all the rests. Get your index cards out and flick them whenever you have a rest as you sing.

Try these warm-ups:

Joshua Fit the Battle

For SAB/3-Part Mixed with Piano

Traditional Spiritual
Arranged by
GREG GILPIN

REHEARSAL SUGGESTIONS FOR
So Take This Song of Joy

Everyone should learn the melody from measure 5-12.

Try switching parts at M14-21.

Singers should try to bring examples from on-line of this melody with different texts.

What do you know about the Shaker religion? Share things you've discovered after a few minutes of research.

Another section where singers can learn the other parts is M44-51. Take some time and each part learn someone else's part.

Use index cards again and flick on rests so that they are a part of the learning. The rests will give the "lilt" or bounce the piece needs throughout.

A nice warm-up for easy singing and to produce the "lilt" needed for this piece would be the following example. Try adding different consonants and using the text as well.

REHEARSAL SUGGESTIONS FOR

A La Nanita Nana
(with Coventry Carol)

Discuss where these two carols came from and perhaps other examples of them as stand alone songs.

What style should one sing a lullaby? What does one do vocally to create a sound suitable as a lullaby?

Sing the entire piece on a "loo" from time to time. Perhaps as a warm-up once the piece is learned. Then change to "doo", then with text or a combination of both. Try having the singers rock their bodies or actually pretend holding a baby in their arms to create the feel and sound.

They dynamics are few but that doesn't mean there can't be dynamic interest. Find the important words in each phrase and bring those out, creating phrasing

Here is a warm-up based on one of the melodies. Work on phrasing, breath support and proper vowels.

REHEARSAL SUGGESTIONS FOR
Let Music Live

Have all the singers learn the solo or melody in measures 9-23. Pay attention to where the rests are and to not breath until the rest. Work on phrasing and find the important syllables and words within each phrase.

What is the form of the piece? Find each section and know the measure numbers.

Rehearse the rhythm at measure 57- 60. What does this rhythm help you feel? Why is the text set to quarter notes at M64? What does rhythm help do in regard to the text?

Is there a *ritard* at measures 66-67? What does the composer do to create the illusion of a *ritard*?

Based on the ideas shared in the text, where do you find "music" within your school, community, country and world?

Try these two warm-ups: